table of contents

Chapter numbers correspond to those in the Handbook for Today's Catholic Teen; *not all chapters are covered.*

section one
DOCTRINE: WHAT DO WE BELIEVE?

section two
PRACTICES

section three
PRAYER AND SOME TRADITIONAL PRAYERS

section four
CATHOLIC MORAL ISSUES
(LIFE IN THE REAL WORLD)

section five
RECORD OF FAITH EXPERIENCES

introduction

This *Activity Notebook* is a companion to the *Handbook for Today's Catholic Teen.* The first four sections will help you connect the material in the *Handbook* to your personal faith experiences, and the fifth section will help you start a permanent record of those experiences.

We've tried to give you a decent amount of space in which to write decent responses, but sometimes a response requires more space than we can afford to give you. We'll mark those questions with a symbol and tell you to respond on a separate sheet of paper.

When you finish answering the questions, you'll notice that most of the writing in the book is yours and that, because your answers cannot be the same as anyone else's, you've actually written a book about your own faith life.

Here are two ways to make your book the best it can be:

- Before you do an activity, read the corresponding pages in the *Handbook*. The *Handbook* page numbers appear in parentheses next to the *Activity Notebook* chapter titles.
- Spend some quality time in your mind with the ideas before you write.

Whether you do these things and how much time you spend on your book is up to you. You can read the *Handbook* and give your responses some real thought, or you can just scribble the first easy words that come to mind, like "love God," "help others," "pray more," "give to the poor," "read the Bible," and the always popular, "Get closer to God." Here's another example:

Q. What do you admire most about Saint Paul?
A. He was holy and spread God's word and did good things, like writing part of the Bible. And he helped people.

There's nothing *wrong* with that answer; it's just that it doesn't say much. Here's a much better answer:

A. He hung in no matter how hard things got. From the start, his preaching often caused him trouble. His life was threatened, and he was beaten up and imprisoned. He could have said, "The heck with this," but he kept hanging in and starting over.

The most important thing to remember as you write is that **this is *your* book.** We hope writing it teaches you some important things about yourself as it helps you grow in your faith.

SECTION ONE

doctrine

what do we believe?

1 if God exists, then what? *(11–12)*

How would *you* complete the sentence, "If God exists, …"? Draw conclusions that make sense to you. Consider the ideas of meaning and purpose in life, hope, goals, and daily living.

Now try the opposite: "If God did *not* exist, …." Avoid easy, obvious endings like, "We wouldn't have to go to church." How would your view of life change? What losses would you feel? How would you feel about growing old(er)? How would you feel about dying?

2 what can we know about God on our own? *(13–14)*

The *Handbook* notes, "Accepting what other people have learned does not mean you're a nonthinking, unquestioning mental sponge."

On a separate sheet of paper, list the areas of knowledge in which you accept and act on what others have learned and taught you—everything from science to soccer, mechanics to medicine. Could be a long list.

Why is it more difficult to accept what others have learned about faith and religion than it is to accept what they've learned about things like astronomy, medicine, or athletics?

3 what is doctrine? *(15)*

What religious beliefs or doctrines are really important to you? Write down all of them, whether they're Catholic or not, and then mark the ones you think are specifically Catholic.

4 where do we get doctrine? revelation *(15–16)*

What major ideas will you tell your young children, things they need to know but are unable to find out on their own at that age? Include any idea that fits this question, not just the religious ideas.

You tell your six-year-old, "Never wander away from home by yourself—it's very dangerous." Your child replies, "I don't believe that. I think that's stupid!" How would you handle this?

Now imagine God's position. God has told us things we need to know and cannot find out by ourselves. But sometimes we say, "I don't think so. Sounds stupid to me." At the same time, God has given us free will and will not violate it. How do you suppose God feels in this situation?

5 the Bible *(16–19)*

Have a Bible handy as you do this section

Almost everyone says we should read the Bible more, but often we don't. What keeps you from reading the Bible more often than you already do? List the reasons on the left and ways to overcome them on the right.

List questions you have about the Bible in general.

Some Bible stories are completely factual; others are not. How would you answer the question, "If the story didn't really happen exactly like it says, what good is it?"

There's probably more discussion and argument about the creation stories and the Adam and Eve story than about any other Bible stories. Read the real thing in Genesis 1—3. What do *you* think are the main points of the stories in those chapters? What truths about God, life, and people are those stories trying to convey?

Skim the *Book of Psalms.* It's full of intense feelings—celebration, joy, guilt, loneliness, fear, and confusion. On a separate sheet of paper, make a two-column list of the psalms you relate to because of the feelings they express.

Psalm number | *What I relate to*

Skim the *Book of Proverbs,* then make a two-column list on a separate sheet of paper **giving specific examples** of the proverbs you find interesting and how they apply to your life.

Proverb | *Meaning for today*

Prayerfully read the following from John 3:16 several times, replacing the phrases *the world* and *everyone who believes in him* with your name:

For God so loved the world that he gave his only Son, so that everyone who believes in him may not perish but may have eternal life. (NRSV)

What feelings does it arouse?

6 Tradition *(20)*

Catholics believe that Sacred Tradition is a source of God's revelation along with the Bible. Briefly, what is Tradition, and how would you answer the question, "But those are just human-made ideas"?

7 faith (and questions and doubt) *(20–22)*

Do you sometimes find yourself saying or thinking, "But how do we *know*…" about items of religion? What do *you* wonder about?

Some people *want* to have doubts about faith. Why?

You may have heard someone say "My faith got me through" a difficult situation or, "If it weren't for my faith, I don't know what I would have done." List some times like that in your life, even if you didn't actually say the words at the time.

"Mature faith is not kindergarten stuff." What do you think that statement means?

Respond to the often-heard statement, "If something can't be *proven,* I'm not going to believe it or accept it."

8 God: a Trinity *(22–23)*

Do you pray most often to God as a Trinity, to the Father, to Jesus the Son, or to the Holy Spirit? (In its official prayers, the Catholic Church does all four.) What topics or concerns are you most comfortable bringing to God as a Trinity, and which ones do you bring to each person individually?

What does knowing that God is a Trinity of three persons—a divine family, so to speak—say to you about the nature of God? (This is pretty abstract, but it's worth working on.)

9 the Father *(23)*

Is it easy for you to relate to God the Father as *Abba...Daddy*? Why or why not?

How could an individual's experience of a *human* father color his or her perception or feeling about *God* the Father?

10 the Son: Jesus Christ *(24–25)*

"Out of love" is the overall reason God the Son became the human being Jesus of Nazareth. What are the three specific reasons?

When we've had an experience just like or similar to another person's, we often say, "I've been *there*." On a separate sheet of paper, make a long list of human experiences—physical, emotional, intellectual, and social; pleasant and unpleasant; exciting and boring—about which almighty God, as Jesus of Nazareth, can truly say, "I've been *there*." How can knowing God has "been there" affect the way we bring our concerns to God in prayer?

11 the Holy Spirit *(25–26)*

The Holy Spirit is often described as acting invisibly behind the scenes to arrange good things and delightful surprises for us. List some times when you believe the Spirit was acting in your life to make things work out or simply to delightfully surprise you.

It's not an accident that the symbols of the Spirit at Pentecost were wind and fire. Think of what wind and fire can do. What does that tell us about the Spirit and what the Spirit can do for us?

12 salvation and redemption *(27–28)*

We sometimes use the words *salvation* and *redemption* almost as synonyms, but they're not quite the same thing. What's the difference?

"*Maybe,* if we're good enough and prove ourselves worthy, we'll be saved and get to heaven." That's not correct. "Jesus redeemed us, so *of course* we'll get to heaven, no matter what—it's a done deal." That's not correct, either. What *is* the correct outlook?

13 grace *(28–30)*

List some times when someone extended a *natural* grace to you—did something good or kind for you for absolutely no reason except that he or she liked you and wanted to.

How do such things mirror, in a small way, God's grace to us?

How are *sanctifying* grace and *actual* grace quite different? What do they have in common—why are they both called *grace*?

Without getting too personal, write about when you are most in need of *actual* grace.

Briefly describe times when *actual* grace helped you do something that was good, but difficult, or when it helped you refuse something that was wrong, but attractive.

14 worship *(30)*

How is worshiping God a matter of looking at reality and responding to it?

If we exist only because God, out of love, *wants* us to exist, why do so many people find it difficult—or even a waste of time—to acknowledge this reality and/or regularly spend time in actual worship?

15 sacraments *(31–33)*

What two things does a sacrament do, and how does that make a sacrament vastly different from an ordinary sign?

Respond to this objection: "Sacraments may work for some people, but not for everybody. Even bloodthirsty dictators, mass murderers, and drug dealers were baptized. Some were confirmed and even received the Eucharist. Sacraments don't work like they're supposed to."

16 baptism *(34–35)*

Have a Bible handy as you do this section

It's easy to take fantastic realities for granted. Life itself, for example. Our status as baptized persons can be like that too. We see baptism as a past event, kind of like, "When I was young, I got my immunization shots." Reflect over and over: "I *am*…a *baptized* person." What meaning does that have for your life right now?

What does the sign of the water of baptism tell us about? What does it actually do?

Slowly read Paul's explanation of baptism in Romans 6:1–11. Remember, you're reading about the way things *really are*. Write your reflections.

17 confirmation *(36–37)*

Try the same reflection with confirmation. What does it mean to remember, "I am a baptized *and confirmed* Catholic Christian"?

Which gift of the Spirit is strongest in you? Which do you most need to develop? Be realistic.

What ideas are in the Greek word *Paraclete*, which we often use to describe the Holy Spirit? Which idea intrigues you the most?

18 reconciliation *(38–39)*

Reconciliation is also known as *penance* or *confession*. What does each term say about what happens in this sacrament?

Some Catholics receive reconciliation regularly, some less often, and some only once in a very long time, while some say, "Oh, I never go (anymore)." Which describes you and why?

If you receive reconciliation very seldom (or haven't for a very long time), what keeps you from doing so? Be gut honest about the reason(s).

19 anointing of the sick *(40)*

Write the names of anyone you know who has received the anointing of the sick and what happened afterward.

The anointing is not only for situations of extreme illness with possible permanent consequences or even death. What other situations can you think of where it would be appropriate to celebrate the anointing of the sick?

20 matrimony *(41–42)*

When we receive the Eucharist or witness baptism or confirmation, we're usually conscious that we are in the presence of something very holy, actually supernatural. Why is it less obvious that *matrimony* is a sacrament, right along with all the others...making Jesus present?

What things tarnish or obscure matrimony's true holiness and make it seem ordinary?

What does the love of husband and wife *reflect* and *channel*? (Two key words.)

List your thoughts on the awesome privilege and responsibility of helping to create new human life—a baby.

What are your hopes and dreams for matrimony, if you are called to it, and what can you do now to help make them happen? Address the whole range of marriage—things beyond family size, careers, homes, vacations, and the other usual topics.

21 holy orders *(43)*

What is the official role of a priest?

What specific powers does a Catholic priest receive in the sacrament of holy orders?

22 Eucharist *(44–46)*

List the names or terms associated with this central sacrament.

What do Catholics *know* happens to the bread and wine at the moment a priest speaks the words of consecration?

23 the Mass *(46–47)*

Outline the basic parts of our Mass as well as you can. If you don't know or remember the official terms, check a missalette or ask your discussion leader and fill in the missing pieces.

Describe a time when a particular Mass was especially meaningful to you or times in general when Mass is meaningful to you now. What makes it that way for you?

Respond to this: "If you don't like the opera or football games, and they don't do anything for you, then don't go to the opera or football games. For people who like them, they're fine. For you, it's a waste of time. It's exactly the same with Mass."

24 the Catholic Church *(48–51)*

Name some things you like about being Catholic.

What, more than anything else, is a distinctively Catholic thing about our faith and worship?

What is the true Catholic outlook about the Catholic Church with regard to other Christian churches?

If you have close friends who belong to other Christian denominations, note their names and the religion or church they belong to. What faith values do you share with them?

____

____

____

25 the afterlife: heaven, hell, and purgatory *(51–53)*

Which of these describes your usual feeling about the afterlife? You may check more than one.

_____ It's way too far off to think about now; I have too many things to do before then.
_____ I don't like to think about it; it makes me a little nervous or, at least, sad.
_____ I can't visualize or imagine it, so why think about it?
_____ God loves us, and it's going to turn out okay anyway, so why think about it?
_____ I hope I have some advance notice; I could use the time to get ready.
_____ Other (write on the lines below)

____

____

_____ And another (write on the lines below)

____

____

What leads you to feel that way? What might change your feelings?

____

____

____

____

If you were to enter the afterlife in five minutes, what would you wish you had done more of or paid more attention to? (Easy opening for comedy. OK, include a couple comedy items, but make the rest serious.)

____

____

____

____

____

____

26 the body of Christ / the communion of saints *(54)*

Describe a time you felt connected with other members of the Church on earth and/or those who are already in the afterlife. (It doesn't have to be a high-powered, mystical experience.) What prompted this? Whom did you feel close to in particular? Can you draw any conclusions?

Reflect on "spiritual connection" among people. What does that phrase mean to you? Does *spiritual* somehow sound less than real—a nice mental idea, but it doesn't actually do much? Or could a *spiritual* connection be the most powerful kind?

What are *your* specific gifts in the body of Christ? What contributions do you make to your community, to the Church, the body of Christ? Really work on this. No generic responses, like "I'm a nice person" or "I like to help people," allowed. Your gifts don't have to be world-shaking or drastically different from everybody else's, but they should be *yours*.

27 Mary *(55–56)*

What do Catholics understand by the following:

Virgin Birth

Immaculate Conception

Assumption

A sincere, non-Catholic friend or acquaintance asks you, "What *do* you Catholics really think about Mary? Why is she a bigger deal to you than she is to other Christians?" How would you answer?

A rugged, all-state linebacker once spoke of his devotion to Mary at a retreat. Among other things, he said, "Mary is…just plain cool." What do you think he meant by that? What would *you* mean by it if you felt and said it?

SECTION TWO

practices

28 sacramentals *(57–58)*

How are sacramentals both similar to and different from things like photographs and mementos of loved ones and important events?

Why are sacramentals *not* superstition or silly, cute religious piety?

What sacramentals do you own or have in your home?

Which sacramentals really say something to you, and why? (They don't have to be things you use or think about every day—one of them could be the once-a-year ashes on Ash Wednesday.)

29 seasons of the liturgical year *(58–61)*

What are the seasons of the liturgical year…in order, beginning with Advent?

Do you have any liturgical-season memories that connect in some way with faith and worship? What are they? Things like candy eggs at Easter don't count; they're tasty, not liturgical. Think prayers, practices, and traditions.

Advent *(58–59)*

Have a Bible handy as you do this section

Advent should be a time of quiet, hopeful waiting for the fulfillment of dreams and promises, but usually we're caught up in preholiday frenzy. Name some ways to recover some of the purpose and spirit of Advent.

What dreams and promises have already been fulfilled in your own life? How did God enter into this?

What dreams and promises are you waiting for now? How is God working it out?

How can your favorite Christmas memories and current Christmas activities remind you that God truly is Emmanuel…"God is with us"? Make some links.

Read the actual Christmas stories or "infancy narratives" of the New Testament (first two chapters of Matthew and Luke) as though you're reading them for the first time. What stood out?

Lent *(59)*

What were your experiences of Lent as a child? Did you give anything up? How do you look back on those practices—as worthwhile then, but now childish and outgrown? Something to build on—or get back to?

Lent calls us to purify ourselves of things that shouldn't be in our lives at all. Think of two or three such things in your life. For privacy, write a code name or a symbol of them on these lines.

If during Lent you were to free yourself, with God's help, of these things (or even make progress toward that), how would you feel about yourself, how would you feel about your relationship with God, and how would your life change?

People who feel intimidated or even helpless to break a bad habit are sometimes able to do it anyway because they keep telling themselves, "*I* can't. *God* can. I think I'll let him." Write your own version of that idea, perhaps in prayer form.

30 **penance *(61–62)***

The phrase "doing penance" has a gloomy image for some people, but for many Catholics it's a joyful thing. Not necessarily easy, but joyful. Describe a time when, for religious or other reasons, you made up for something you had done wrong and felt much better than you would have if you had simply tried to forget it.

What would be a good penance for you personally at this time of your life (and how can you avoid putting it off)?

31 **receiving reconciliation *(62–63)***

When was a time you experienced and deeply felt forgiveness—you *knew* from some tangible sign or event that you were forgiven, and you felt renewed, refreshed, and ready to start over?

Do you sometimes think you would receive reconciliation and get some things out and over with if it were easier to do so? What would make it easier—and likely to happen?

32 receiving Communion *(64–65)*

Receiving Communion should not be difficult or accompanied by fear that we're not doing it right. However, a distracted, "Oh, yeah—time to go up and get Communion now," while we're thinking of other things isn't right, either. Reflect on your current way of receiving Communion. Could you prepare yourself better…show greater reverence…make it mean more?

In the past, receiving Communion was seen as a private experience. We now realize that the Eucharist is a community, family event. But have we lost sight of the personal, physical presence of Jesus within us during the moments after Communion? How can you combine the elements of community and a personal encounter with Jesus? How can you best spend the moments after receiving Communion?

33 holy days of obligation *(66)*

For some, these days have sunk to, "Oh, well, nobody does that anymore." Actually, many people do, and they're not just "old people who have nothing else to do but go to church." What benefit, what *grace* lies in making special feast days holy through worship?

34-35 the corporal (material or physical) and spiritual works of mercy *(67–70)*

Fill one column with the works of mercy you currently do and the other with possibilities that interest you or that are needed by someone you know. Look at each one imaginatively. Take credit for what you're already doing; then stretch your vision toward further possibilities.

	Already Doing	Possibilites
Corporal Feed the hungry. Give drink to the thirsty.		
Clothe the naked.		
Visit those in prison.		
Shelter the homeless.		
Visit the sick.		

Bury the dead.

Spiritual

Instruct the ignorant.

Admonish the sinner.

Counsel the doubtful.

Comfort the sorrowful.

Bear wrongs patiently.
Forgive all injuries.

Pray for the living
and the dead.

SeCtioN ThrEE

prayer

and some traditional prayers

36 what prayer is *(71–72)*

Any conversation, including prayer, is colored by how you see yourself and how you see the person you're conversing with. When you pray, how do you see yourself and God? Do you "see" or feel different things when you pray in different circumstances?

Some people (not just monks and nuns) have definite prayer times. Others pray briefly here and there all day long or whenever the thought comes to mind. Many people do both, and spiritual advisors say we should. What is your pattern of prayer, and how could it be expanded or improved?

Even people who firmly believe that all prayer does some good can have trouble feeling that *their* particular prayer is worthwhile or will have some effect. On a scale of one to ten, rate the amount of good you think prayer does. What events that *did or didn't* happen led you to that rating?

We sometimes (maybe even usually) skip the *listening* part of prayer. Maybe it's because we don't really expect an answer, figure the answer will come later, or are simply in a hurry. (And maybe we don't want to hear God's answer.) What's your experience of listening in prayer?

37 why pray? *(73–74)*

What aspects of your life (usually things that are going rather well) might tempt you to think that, at least for right now, you don't need prayer that much?

Other side of the coin: What aspects of your life indicate that you *do* need to pray?

The *Handbook* mentions "ought to" and "need to" as two main reasons for "why pray?" and then mentions a "want to" dimension. When have you truly wanted to pray? When do you truly want to pray now? (Situations such as needing to be rescued from a pack of snarling Doberman pinschers don't count.)

38 types of prayer *(74–75)*

Praise and adoration. Fervent fans of earthly celebrities easily tell their heroes that they're wonderful, awesome, etc. Such words don't always leap out as spontaneously and naturally toward God. Create some of your own. Talk to God about God and God's works. You don't have to be literary. You just have to mean it.

Thanksgiving. On a separate sheet of paper, make a list of one hundred things you're grateful for. Let your mind wander over the terrain of your life, past and present, and write things just as you think of them. Don't be concerned with putting things into categories or trying to follow a logical order—you can do that later if you choose. If you're like most young people who've undertaken this activity, you'll probably find you're well beyond one hundred things and into *several hundred* things.

Keep your list and reread it every now and then, adding a few things to it each time. Some people keep their list on the computer so they can insert the new items in order of importance. It's a great way to remind yourself of the treasures you really do have in your life but take for granted.

Petition. Most of us are beyond the, "Please send me a puppy or a pony for my birthday, a pony would be better," stage of prayer. When God invited Solomon to ask for whatever gift he wanted (1 Kings 3:5–10), Solomon asked for "an understanding mind," for wisdom. Thinking along those lines, what gift(s) would you ask for so you can be the kind of person you really *want* to be?

____

____

____

____

Reparation or contrition. The things we most regret are usually also the most personal and not easy to describe in words. Use this space to draw symbols of things you are genuinely sorry for, and perhaps symbols of your intentions to do better. Only you have to know what they mean. God already does.

Read the prayer-starter section on page 75 of the *Handbook*; then list some things that would make good prayer starters for *you*.

____

____

____

Prayer sites abound on the Internet; for example, Sacred Space (www.sacredspace.ie) has a daily prayer in numerous languages, a Lenten retreat, and other ways to pray. Do a prayer-site search of your own and list some of your favorite sites here.

39 prayer to Mary and the saints *(76–77)*

Why *do* Catholics pray to Mary in particular and to other saints? How would you explain this practice to a non-Catholic who is confused by it—maybe even pretty negative about it? See the *Handbook* for the beginning of an explanation; then continue it in your own words.

The Internet abounds with Catholic saint sites. Do an Internet search for saints. Browse for patron saints of careers, activities, or hobbies that interest you. Which saints caught your interest?

40 traditional prayers *(78)*

Which traditional prayers do you say most often?

Have you ever found yourself suddenly forming the words of a traditional prayer, almost without thinking, because of some sudden happening or circumstance?

42 Our Father (the Lord's Prayer) *(79)*

Fill the phrases of the Our Father with the meaning and associations it has for your own life:

Our Father, who art in heaven,

hallowed be thy name;

thy kingdom come;

thy will be done on earth as it is in heaven.

Give us this day our daily bread;

and forgive us our trespasses

as we forgive those who trespass against us;

and lead us not into temptation,

but deliver us from evil.

49 morning offering *(86)*

"There's my spiritual, religious life, like when I pray, and then there's my regular, ordinary life, which is all the rest of it—which is practically all of it." No. The morning offering is a great way to be reminded that we *don't* live on two separate tracks, switching only occasionally and very briefly from ordinary to spiritual. "Let it [my day, united with Jesus] be *a force for helping good things happen* throughout the world," this version of the morning offering prays.

Explore this idea on the lines below. Link the ordinary stuff of your life with benefits it can help make happen in the world. Some examples:

Ordinary activity	**Benefit to others**
Waking up, getting started when you don't feel like it	Strength for someone who doesn't feel he/she can get through another day
Trying to get something out of first bell	Opportunity for someone who desperately needs an education to do so
Lunch with friends	Greater awareness of our obligations to those who face starvation

Section Four

Catholic moral issues

(life in the real world)

53 moral behavior and the life of faith *(89–90)*

The subtitle of this section is "life in the real world," that is, living as a Catholic Christian among the real people and circumstances we're part of, choosing right over wrong. But often that phrase "real world" is used to describe a life in *contrast* to the life and behavior of faith—as though there's the "faith world" (the way things *should* be), and then there's the "real world," which is how things *actually are*.

Do you think we sometimes use, "But in the *real* world…" as an excuse for not living as we *should*—and *could*? What are your thoughts about living as a Catholic Christian in the "real world?"

54 temptation *(90–91)*

To have a realistic approach to temptation, we need to be clear about three things. What are they?

In your opinion, what are the most common temptation situations a person might put himself or herself in, vaguely assuming that "nothing bad will happen," and then later say, "I couldn't help it—I was surrounded and overwhelmed by temptation"?

55 sin *(91–93)*

Catholics have been accused of being entirely too "sin conscious" in the past. Maybe so, maybe not; in either case, that was the past. Where are we today? *Do* Catholics think about sin too much, exactly as much as we should, or not nearly enough? Why do you say that?

A few people have a rare physical condition in which their nerve endings are so insensitive that they seldom feel physical pain. That *sounds* good, but it's a dangerous situation because they get no warning when something is physically very wrong; for example, if they're near something dangerously hot, they don't feel it, so they don't move away, and they get burned. It's been said that seldom feeling guilt is a similarly dangerous spiritual condition. Agree or disagree? Why?

The *Handbook* says it's probably easier to drift little by little into a state of mortal sin than to get there by one single action. What do *you* think?

Assuming that someone can indeed drift gradually into a state of mortal sin, what begins the drift? What things in a person's life—or what *lack*—begin the slide downward and keep it going?

56 conscience *(93–94)*

We often hear statements like, "You should follow your conscience. If you *think* something is wrong for you, then it *is* wrong for you. And if you *think* something is right for you, then it *is* right for you. *You* have to decide for yourself. Everybody's different."

No doubt, you need to follow your conscience. As for the rest, certainly there's some truth there, but if that's the whole story on conscience and behavior, we have big problems. Murder might be wrong for *some* people but "right" for others. What part of the statements in the previous paragraph is the simple truth, what part needs a whole lot of explanation, and what part is just plain missing?

When we want to learn how to do something well and correctly, we look to people who have been there before and who know the territory. Why is this an easy method to accept in, let's say, physics—but not so easy in morality?

57 the Ten Commandments *(95–96)*

It's worth rereading the brief sections in the *Handbook* of what each commandment covers. It's usually obvious which bad things would *not* happen if everyone kept the commandments, so let's go beyond that. For each commandment, list some *good* things, positive results, and rich benefits that happen when people *keep* that commandment.

1.

2.

3.

4.

5.

6.

7.

8.

9.

10.

58 the law of love *(97–98)*

How *can* we genuinely love someone we don't like or even positively can't stand? What does loving such a person mean and involve?

What are some common ideas about love that are false or at least incomplete?

Find creative, colorful—and sound—ways to complete the sentence, "You know someone *really* loves you when…" (one or two comedy items are allowed, but keep the rest serious).

59 the problem of evil *(99–100)*

What events or conditions have you personally experienced or simply heard about that prompted *you* to raise the question, "How can God let that happen?"

more lines on next page

When tragedy happens, you may hear someone say, "Everything happens for a reason," or "God must have a reason behind it all." Is this just a superficial way of defending God or faith in God? Is it well meant but not accurate? Is there *any* truth in it?

We believe God can bring good out of evil. Within your personal experience and that of your family or close friends, how have you seen this happen?

60 the world: run away or blend in? *(100–102)*

The *Handbook* describes two opposite attitudes, both of them wrong, toward a world that frequently does not operate on Christian values. *Why* is each of them wrong?

"You should believe in your faith, but you can't be a freak about it." Any truth to that? Any error in it?

Few people actually say it, but a common fear about living a thoroughly Catholic Christian life is that it will make you look or act weird and spoil your fun. What are your *honest* feelings about this?

"There are some things we simply cannot do, some lifestyles we simply cannot adopt, and still say we're following Jesus." What are some of them (besides obvious things like serial killing and bank robbing)?

61 the media *(102)*

"Sure, I watch that stuff and listen to it, but it doesn't affect how I think." Psychologists say that's like saying, "Sure, I walk around in air that has dust in it, but I never get any dust on my skin." How much influence does the media have in your life? In what ways does this influence show itself to you and others?

A common observation about the entertainment culture is that when something is funny, entertaining, or cleverly written and performed, people look at it and think it's OK. Maybe they don't actually *say* it's OK, but they soak that idea in little by little. Entertainment makes wrong things look either OK or at least not so bad. Your honest thoughts on this:

What *good* things are happening in the media—things that directly or indirectly foster the values of Jesus?

62 violence *(103)*

Our culture has been criticized for glorifying violence in everything from films to lyrics to video and computer games. Defenders usually say one of three things in response: 1) it's *just* a movie (song, game, etc.); 2) that's how things are—it's reality; 3) *seeing* violence doesn't make you *be* violent—that's *your* choice.

Think critically about those defenses. Do they really produce the conclusion, "Well, in that case, there's no harm done"?

more lines on next page

Describe two of the most peaceful, nonviolent people you know: one whom you know personally and one whom you know about. Do they come across to you as weak because of their peaceful nature…or strong?

63 honesty *(104)*

Describe one of the most honest people you know. What positive feelings do you get from knowing this person, even if you don't always get along?

"It would be *nice* to be completely honest all the time, but it doesn't work. There's no way you can get what you need to succeed and be happy if you're totally honest in everything." Agree or disagree? (If it's true, *every successful, happy person is also a cheat and a liar.*)

64 sexuality *(105–106)*

The *Handbook* says that God's rules about sex are not simply tests of obedience or unnecessary restrictions on enjoyment, but also ways of steering us toward genuine happiness—and that the evidence shows that for every small amount of temporary pleasure in sex outside of marriage, there are huge amounts of eventual harm, sorrow, and regret. Looking honestly at the facts of human experience, what do *you* think?

more lines on next page

Over and over in Scripture, God tells us enthusiastically what a good thing our sexuality is. The love of a husband for his wife is used as an image of God's love for God's people. A wedding banquet is used as a symbol of the celebration of the kingdom of God. But many people have a real problem linking God, holiness, and sex. Why?

The virtue of chastity means saving the gift of sex to celebrate the love of marriage and, within marriage, remaining faithful to one's spouse. A common view of chastity is, "Nice idea, but let's get real." What do *you* think?

Do you think some young people give up on the idea of chastity (even though on their own they would prefer it) because they've grown up being told by our culture that it's either impossible or weird? Have they been pressured into thinking, "It must be true…I *can't* say no"?

65 alcohol and drugs *(106–108)*

The disastrous results of alcohol and drug abuse are massively and monstrously obvious. The evidence is mountainous and inescapable. Yet thousands and thousands of people get involved in them anyway. Obviously, simply knowing about the dangers and consequences is very little protection. What *does* keep people from abusing drugs and alcohol?

SECTION FIVE

record of faith experiences

People of faith are storytellers. The Israelites of the Hebrew Scriptures (Old Testament) and the Christians of the New Testament recorded their experiences of faith and their relationship with God. Through those records, God revealed his truth to them and to us.

You also have a faith story to tell. This section of your *Activity Notebook* is designed for you to record the basic nuggets of important experiences in your faith life. Looking back on these experiences will renew and refresh your faith in the same way pictures from a family vacation, school activity, or prom remind you of how good the experience was and how important to you the people involved were.

Don't be concerned with writing style—just concentrate on remembering and describing the details. You're writing this for *yourself,* not for someone else.

sacraments

baptism

Unless you were baptized later in life, you don't remember your baptism, but other people probably do. Ask them about it.

Name of church:

Names of godparents and their relationship to you:

Details:

first Communion

We celebrate the sacrament of the Eucharist many times, but the very first time is a special occasion. What do you remember about it?

more lines on next page

confirmation

Name of your sponsor and why you chose him or her:

Name of bishop:

Confirmation name and why you chose it:

Confirmation-preparation and confirmation Mass memories:

reconciliation

Note the especially meaningful or joyful times you received reconciliation (for example, at a retreat).

more lines on next page

spiritual experiences

The term *spiritual experiences* doesn't mean floating on some kind of mysterious, mystical cloud. It refers to things like retreats; talks on a spiritual theme; a special homily; a class or seminar; a special liturgy; an event that prompted you to search for meaning, even a sad event like the death of a grandparent; a time or period of prayer that was especially rewarding and enlightening; something you read that connected with or strengthened your faith; an enlightening or encouraging conversation.

church-related activities and service to others

These two go together because a church-related activity often involves service. This section covers everything from attending a youth-group dance to working at a soup kitchen to going on a mission trip. Besides recording just the essential facts—what, when, where, with whom—note what you learned from it, whom you helped, and how it and they helped *you*.

Editor: Maureen Connolly
Cover design: Jodi Hendrickson
Cover image: Comstock

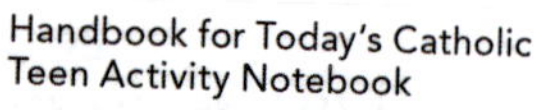

ISBN 978-0-764-81378-8